THE
PASSIONATE
LIFE

BIBLE STUDY SERIES

Galatians
HEAVEN'S
FREEDOM

10-WEEK STUDY GUIDE

BroadStreet
P U B L I S H I N G

BroadStreet Publishing Group, LLC
Racine, Wisconsin, USA
BroadStreetPublishing.com

The Passionate Life Bible Study Series
GALATIANS: HEAVEN'S FREEDOM 10-WEEK STUDY GUIDE

Edited by Jeremy Bouma

ISBN-13: 978-1-4245-5329-7 (soft cover)
ISBN-13: 978-1-4245-5330-3 (e-book)

To purchase any of the study guides in the The Passionate Life Bible Study Series in bulk for use in groups, please send an email to orders@broadstreetpublishing.com.

Cover design by Chris Garborg at GarborgDesign.com
Typesetting by Katherine Lloyd at theDESKonline.com

Printed in the United States of America

16 17 18 19 20 5 4 3 2 1

Contents

Using the Passionate Life Bible Study

The psalmist declares, "Truth's shining light guides me in my choices and decisions; the revelation of your Word makes my pathway clear" (Psalm 119:105).

This verse forms the foundation of The Passionate Life Bible Study series. Not only do we want to kindle within you a deep, burning passion for God and his Word, but we also want to let the Word's light blaze a bright path before you to help you make truth-filled choices and decisions, while encountering the heart of God along the way.

God longs to have his Word expressed in a way that unlocks the passion of his heart for the reader. Inspired by The Passion Translation but usable with any Bible translation, this is a heart-level Bible study, from the passion of God's heart to the passion of your heart. Our goal is to trigger inside you an overwhelming response to the truth of the Bible.

DISCOVER. EXPLORE. EXPERIENCE. SHARE.

Each of the following lessons is divided into four sections: *Discover the Heart of God; Explore the Heart of God; Experience the Heart of God;* and *Share the Heart of God.* They are meant to guide your study of the truth of God's Word, while drawing you closer and deeper into his passionate heart for you and your world.

The *Discover* section is designed to help you make observations about the reading. Every lesson opens with the same three questions: What did you notice, perhaps for the first time? What questions do you have? And, what did you learn about the heart of God? There are no right answers here! They are meant to jump-start your journey into God's truth by bringing to the surface your initial impressions about the passage. The other questions help draw your attention to specific points the author wrote and discover the truths God is conveying.

Explore takes you deeper into God's Word by inviting you to think more critically and explain what the passage is saying. Often there is some extra information to highlight and clarify certain aspects of the passage, while inviting you to make connections. Don't worry if the answers aren't immediately apparent. Sometimes you may need to dig a little deeper or take a little more time to think. You'll be grateful you did, because you will have tapped into God's revelation-light in greater measure!

Experience is meant to help you do just that: experience God's heart for you personally. It will help you live out God's Word by applying it to your unique life situation. Each question in this section is designed to bring the Bible into your world in fresh, exciting, and relevant ways. At the end of this section, you will have a better idea of how to make choices and decisions that please God, while walking through life on clear paths bathed in the light of his revelation!

The final section is *Share*. God's Word isn't meant to be merely studied or memorized; it's meant to be shared with other people—both through living and telling. This section helps you understand how the reading relates to growing closer to others, to enriching your fellowship and relationship with your world. It also helps you listen to the stories of those around you, so you can bridge Jesus' story with their stories.

SUGGESTIONS FOR INDIVIDUAL STUDY

Reading and studying the Bible is an exciting journey! This study is designed to help you encounter the heart of God and let his Word to you reach deep down into your very soul—all so you can live and enjoy the life he intends for you. And like with any journey, a number of practices will help you along the way:

1. Begin your lesson time in prayer, asking God to open up his Word to you in new ways, show areas of your heart that need teaching

and healing, and correct any area in which you're living contrary to his desires for your life.

2. Read the opening section to gain an understanding of the major themes of the reading and ideas for each lesson.

3. Read through the Scripture passage once, underlining or noting in your Bible anything that stands out to you. Reread the passage again, keeping in mind these three questions: What did you notice, perhaps for the first time? What questions do you have? What did you learn about the heart of God?

4. Write your answers to the questions in this Bible study guide or a notebook. If you do get stuck, first ask God to reveal his Word to you and guide you in his truth. And then, either wait until your small group time or ask a trusted leader for help.

5. Use the end of the lesson to focus your time of prayer, thanking and praising God for the truth of his Word, for what he has revealed to you, and for how he has impacted your daily life.

SUGGESTIONS FOR SMALL GROUP STUDY

The goal of this study is to understand God's Word for you and your community in greater measure, while encountering his heart along the way. A number of practices will help your group as you journey together:

1. Group studies usually go better when everyone is prepared to participate. The best way to prepare is to come having read the lesson's Scripture reading beforehand. Following the suggestions in each individual study will enrich your time as a community as well.

2. Before you begin the study, your group should nominate a leader to guide the discussion. While this person should work through the questions beforehand, his or her main job isn't to lecture, but to

help move the conversation along by asking the lesson questions and facilitating the discussion.

3. Encourage everyone to share. Be sure to listen well, contribute where you feel led, and try not to dominate the conversation.

4. The number one rule for community interaction is: nothing is off-limits! No question is too dumb; no answer is out of bounds. While many questions in this study have "right" answers, most are designed to push you and your friends to explore the passage more deeply and understand what it means for daily living.

5. Finally, be ready for God to reveal himself through the passage being discussed and through the discussion that arises out of the group he's put together. Pray that he would reveal his heart and revelation-light to you all in deeper ways. And be open to being challenged, corrected, and changed.

Again, we pray and trust that this Bible study will kindle in you a burning, passionate desire for God and his heart, while impacting your life for years to come. May it open wide the storehouse of heaven's revelation-light. May it reveal new and greater insights into the mysteries of God and the king-dom-realm life he has for you. And may you encounter the heart of God in more fresh and relevant ways than you ever thought possible!

Introduction to Galatians

If you are searching for true freedom—freedom from sin, from shame and guilt, even from death itself—look no further than Galatians. In it we find the revelation-truth of Paul's "grace gospel," which proclaims heaven's freedom for every believer. Our hope no longer rests with keeping religious laws, but dwells now in Christ. We have a grace-righteousness that places us at the right hand of the throne of God as sons and daughters of the Most High.

When Paul wrote his letter proclaiming heaven's freedom, the grace gospel was under attack. There were people who were perverting his original message of rescue from sin and death by grace through faith in Christ alone. They added religious works to Paul's gospel, but the grace gospel brings heaven's freedom from religious bondage. Thanks to Paul, we are reminded that the gospel is Christ and Christ alone, without anything added. We are called to use that freedom to produce fruit by the power of the Spirit. Since Paul received his message through a direct encounter with Jesus, his gospel can be trusted and believed.

This study is designed to help you explore and discover God's heart for the world through reading and embracing Paul's revelation of his gospel of grace. May the Lord bring his glory and freedom into your heart as you encounter the heart of God through this heaven-inspired letter to the Galatians. Take it as the gospel truth.

Lesson 1

No Other Gospel but the Grace Gospel

GALATIANS 1:1–10

There is only one gospel—
the gospel of the Messiah! (Galatians 1:7)

Our day is a day of multiple "gospels." There's the "gospel" that says God saves people from monetary ruin and offers financial prosperity. Another "gospel" saves people from social injustice and corrupt human systems. Yet another "gospel" requires performing certain religious rituals in order to be saved. In reality, these Jesus-plus-something gospels are all false.

The true gospel is radically different. It is a Jesus-plus-nothing gospel all the way! This isn't a gospel of salvation by works, it doesn't right social wrongs, and it isn't about financial blessing. These are all distortions of the only true gospel—the gospel of the Messiah, who came to earth to take away the sins of the world by paying our price and taking our place.

If Paul were alive today, he'd tell us the same thing he wrote the Galatian Christians: "I am shocked over how quickly you have deserted the grace gospel and strayed away from the Anointed One who called you to himself by his loving mercy" (1:6). Galatians unfolds for us crucial revelation-insights

11

about the gospel that are vital to every believer. There is no other gospel but the grace gospel.

Discover the Heart of God

- After reading Galatians 1:1–10, what did you notice, perhaps for the first time? What questions do you still have? What did you learn about the heart of God?

- The word *apostle* means "one who is sent on a mission" or "an ambassador." By implication, an apostle carries the delegated authority of the one who sends him. Who was the apostle Paul, and from where did he claim his authority?

- What has the anointed Messiah done for every Christian?

- Why was Paul "shocked" at the Galatian Christians?

- How did Paul say Christians should respond to "a different message than the grace gospel" (1:8)?

Explore the Heart of God

- Why did Paul write this letter to the Christians throughout central Turkey? Why was it important that Paul claimed that his authority to write such a letter was from the anointed Messiah, Jesus Christ?

- What is the "grace gospel"? How had the Galatian Christians deserted it?

- Why did Paul curse those (even angels!) who come with a message other than the grace gospel?

• Paul wanted to be clear in his letter, so he said, "Anyone, no matter who they are, that brings you a different gospel than the grace gospel that you have received, let them be condemned and cursed" (1:9). How does this amplify the reason Paul wrote this letter?

• Why wouldn't Paul be a true servant of the Messiah if all he attempted to do was please people? How did this relate to his reason for writing his letter in the first place?

Experience the Heart of God

- How have you personally experienced the grace gospel that Paul speaks about in 1:3–5?

- In what ways do people often embrace a gospel of works like the Galatians did? How does embracing such a distorted gospel impact your experience of the heart of God?

- Has anyone ever come to you with a different gospel than the grace gospel? What was that like? What should be your response, based on 1:8–9?

Share the Heart of God

- After his resurrection and before his ascension, Jesus said, "All the authority of the universe has been given to me. Now go in my authority" (Matthew 28:18–19). Why does this authority of Christ, the anointed Messiah, matter when we share the heart of God, just as it did for Paul?

- In what ways do people today water down the message of the grace gospel when they share the heart of God with others? How can you maintain your supreme passion in pleasing God as you share his heart with others while avoiding the temptation to please people?

- When you share the heart of God by sharing the grace gospel, what should you say so that it isn't distorted? Who is one person you can share this marvelous news with this week?

CONSIDER THIS

Paul is right: there is only one gospel. It isn't about financial prosperity and blessing; it isn't about legalistic religious regulations; it isn't even primarily about righting unjust social systems. First and foremost, the true gospel is about the grace of God, through the Messiah, taking away the sins of the world. If people tell us differently, "let them be condemned and cursed" (1:9).

Lesson 2

The No-Man's Gospel of Jesus, the Anointed One

GALATIANS 1:11–2:10

Beloved ones, let me say emphatically that the gospel
entrusted to me was not given to me by any man.
No one taught me this revelation, for it was given to me directly
by the unveiling of Jesus the Anointed One before my eyes.
(Galatians 1:11–12)

What do all of the false, distorted gospels have in common? They all originate with people. Not so, however, with the grace gospel. This gospel of grace sits at the heart of Galatians, which focuses on heaven's freedom for every believer.

Today's lesson is important because, as Paul reveals in our opening verse, "the gospel entrusted to me was not given to me by any man" (1:11). So where did it come from? It came from Jesus, the Anointed One.

As Paul relates in Acts 9, Jesus himself called Paul (who was then named Saul). He recounts this story of radical transformation in our reading for this lesson. He also reveals something crucial to our understanding of the gospel. God unfolded the grace of Jesus in Paul and entrusted to him the task of proclaiming the grace gospel of heaven's freedom to the non-Jewish people. This message was affirmed by early church leaders and has been going out into the world ever since.

Paul reminds us that the grace gospel of the Anointed One is radically different from the other "gospels" of our day. The grace gospel is a no-man's gospel.

Discover the Heart of God

- After reading Galatians 1:11–2:10, what did you notice, perhaps for the first time? What questions do you still have? What did you learn about the heart of God?

- Who entrusted to Paul the grace gospel? Why is Paul so specific about where he did *not* receive the revelation of the grace gospel?

- What happened to Paul that radically changed his life? What did Paul do afterward? What did the Jewish believers recognize about Paul after his transformation?

- What clear revelation did God give Paul that compelled him to meet with the apostolic leaders?

- How did Christian leaders in Jerusalem react to Paul's grace message? How did false "brothers" in Judea react? What did Christian leaders in Jerusalem ultimately conclude about Paul's message and ministry?

Explore the Heart of God

- Why did Paul say emphatically that the gospel entrusted to him "was not given to me by any man" (1:11)? Why was this important to his ministry?

- Why did Paul recount his conversion and post-conversion stories? How does this retelling connect to his earlier statement in 1:11–12? What does Paul's conversion story tell us about the heart of God?

- What did Paul mean in 1:15 when he wrote, "God called me by his grace; and in love, he chose me from my birth to be his"? How does this apply to all Christians today?

- Why was it important for Paul to confer with other apostles concerning the message of grace he was preaching to non-Jews?

- Why was it significant that the Jewish Christians in Jerusalem accepted Titus without demanding that he follow strict Jewish customs?

Experience the Heart of God

- Consider your own story of conversion. How has God changed your life through the gospel of grace in Christ?

- What does it mean to you that, like Paul, God called you by his grace and chose you from birth to be his? What does this say about God's heart toward you?

- How have you witnessed Christians trying to bring you or others back into a legalistic bond? How are false "brothers" nowadays adulterating and changing the grace gospel, though perhaps in different ways?

- How should "the wonderful liberty and freedom that we have in Jesus the Anointed One" (2:4) impact your experience of the heart of God?

Share the Heart of God

- Why does it matter that the gospel we share hasn't been given to us by anyone but Jesus, the Anointed One?

- How can our own conversion stories and ongoing transformation be used of God for his glory when we share his heart? How might he want to use yours?

- When Paul began sharing the heart of God, he submitted his message before other Christians for evaluation and scrutiny. Why might this be important for you as you share God's heart in the gospel of grace, as believers did in Paul's day?

- Paul revealed that just as God gave Peter a special ministry to Jews, he had also given Paul a special ministry to non-Jews. Whom might God specifically be giving to you to share his heart and the grace gospel?

CONSIDER THIS

The good news of God's love for the world in Jesus, which has set at the heart of the Christian faith for two millennia, isn't human news. It wasn't manufactured by men, or hammered and honed by humans. The revelation of the grace gospel came from God. Not only that, this grace gospel has been entrusted to every one of us by Jesus Christ himself.

Lesson 3

———

Die to Your Religious Identity

GALATIANS 2:11-21

My old identity has been crucified with the Messiah
and no longer lives; for the nails of his cross crucified me
with him.And now the essence of this new life is no longer mine,
for the Anointed One lives his life through me—
we live in union as one! (Galatians 2:20)

What makes you who you are? How do you identify yourself? Perhaps you're a truck driver, a small business owner, or a nurse. If you're living in the western world, you might be American or Australian or Canadian. Sometimes religious people identify themselves as Baptist or Lutheran.

Regardless of how you identify yourself, Paul teaches us an important truth: When we were saved by grace through faith in Christ, we died to our old identities—especially our religious identities. Now we aren't the ones living our lives; Christ lives in and through us. Our acceptance by God in Christ affects every ounce of our identities. As Paul revealed, our old selves were nailed to the cross along with Christ—including our old *religious* selves. That's a lesson Peter needed to learn—a lesson Paul was quick to give.

Today we learn, along with Peter, that in turning to Christ in faith, we have given up on identifying as a religious person and orienting our lives around fulfilling religious laws. We've also set aside our old identity with sin and death now that we've died with Christ, so that we live for him and in his power.

Discover the Heart of God

- After reading Galatians 2:11–21, what did you notice, perhaps for the first time? What questions do you still have? What did you learn about the heart of God?

- What did Peter do when he visited Antioch? Why did Paul oppose him to his face? What did Paul say Peter's example in Antioch condoned?

- What's the reason we receive God's perfect righteousness? Why *don't* we receive it?

- Does God accept those who keep religious laws? Whom does he accept?

- What did Paul say we do when we turn to religious systems? What happened when Paul tried to obey the Law? Why did Paul say he died to it? What happened to Paul's old identity when he died to the Law?

• Why doesn't Paul view God's grace as minor or peripheral?

Explore the Heart of God

• Why was it necessary for Paul to confront Peter's behavior over misleading the believers in Antioch? What was hypocritical about how Peter was acting? Why was it a poor example?

• In what way wasn't Peter being honest about what he believed? How was he "acting inconsistently with the revelation of grace" (2:14)?

- What did Paul mean when he suggested that we don't receive God's perfect righteousness as a reward for keeping the Law?

- In 2:16, the Aramaic and Greek both clearly say "the faith of Jesus, the Messiah." Salvation is found in the "faith of Jesus." How has the faithfulness of Christ saved us and provided us with God's perfect righteousness?

- What did Paul mean by saying, "If I start over and reconstruct the old religious system that I have torn down with the message of grace, I will appear to be one who turns his back on the truth" (2:18)?

Experience the Heart of God

- What sorts of misleading teachings threaten believers today, just as believers were threatened with the distorted gospel of works in Antioch?

- What are some ways Christians behave legalistically and hypocritically? How can you guard against this in your life?

- How do you think it would look to act "inconsistently with the revelation of grace" (2:14)? How might that stand in the way of experiencing the heart of God?

• In what way would it impact your daily experience of God's heart if you believed, deep down, that God has accepted you purely by his grace and not by your keeping religious laws? How should the truth that "we don't receive God's perfect righteousness as a reward for keeping the law" (2:16) impact that experience?

• Paul said that we've been "crucified with the Messiah" (2:20). In what specific ways do you want your union with Christ to impact your life? How do you need him to dispense his life into yours?

Share the Heart of God

- In recent surveys, *hypocrite* has ranked among the top three descriptors of Christians by non-Christians. How might hypocrisy threaten your ability to share the heart of God with those you know?

- Why is it such good news to those with whom we share the heart of God that we've "died to the law's dominion over [us] so that [we] can live for God" (2:19)? What does this mean for your friends and family?

- How do you think people will react to the reality that "we don't receive God's perfect righteousness as a reward for keeping the law, but by the faith of Jesus the Messiah" (2:16)?

- Whom do you know who needs the life of Christ "dispensed" into them? How might you share the heart of God with them to meet this need?

CONSIDER THIS

How do you identify yourself religiously? Are you a Protestant or a Catholic? An Evangelical or an Episcopalian? Or are you simply a Christian—a "little Christ," as the word means literally? While denominational affiliation is okay, sometimes it can lead to what Peter struggled with: religiosity in addition to our relationship with Christ. Let's follow Paul's advice by acting consistently with the revelation of grace by dying to our old identities—even religious ones.

Lesson 4

Not What We Do, What God Did

GALATIANS 3:1–14

*God's plan all along was to bring this message of salvation
to the nations through the revelation of faith.* (Galatians 3:8)

From the beginning of time, people have been trying to appease a deity. These efforts have included prayers and mantras, fasting and other forms of self-denial, or ritualistic sacrifices, beginning with animals and escalating to humans—even to children. What we find in the revelation-truth of the grace gospel, however, is something profoundly different. "No one achieves the righteousness of God by attempting to keep the law" (3:11). It's not what we do for God, but what God did for us in the Messiah.

That's what Paul unfolds before us in today's lesson. God's plan from the beginning was that people would be rescued through the revelation of grace through faith, not through the legalistic rules of religion. Paul even reveals that when we try to reconstruct such legalistic religious systems, we actually deconstruct the grace gospel. And if we could become right with God through keeping religious laws, then Jesus died for nothing.

Paul reveals the fascinating truth that Jesus did all that was necessary to make us right with God. May this lesson open you up to greater revelation-truth and into the secrets of the *Jesus-plus-nothing* grace gospel.

Discover the Heart of God

- After reading Galatians 3:1–14, what did you notice, perhaps for the first time? What questions do you still have? What did you learn about the heart of God?

- How has the Holy Spirit come to us believers? How has he been poured out upon us?

- When does our new life in the Anointed One begin? How is every believer brought to maturity in the Anointed One?

- Why was God's righteousness and salvation released to Abraham? What did Paul say was God's plan all along regarding this salvation?

- What happens when people choose to live under the legalistic rule of religion? What does keeping the law require?

• What did Paul say that the Messiah, our anointed substitute, has done for us?

Explore the Heart of God

• How had the Galatian Christians acted "stupidly," "missed the revelation of truth" (3:1), and turned "from living in the Spirit to becoming slaves again to [their] flesh" (3:3)?

• What are the benefits we've received because of the outpouring of the Holy Spirit upon us? List them here.

- What did Paul mean by "the law"? What was it? Why is it true that people live under the law's curse if they choose to live in bondage under the legalistic rule of religion? Why don't people achieve the righteousness of God by attempting to keep the law?

- What did Paul mean when he said the "blessing of Abraham's faith is now our blessing too" (3:9)?

- How did our anointed substitute, Jesus the Messiah, pay the full price to set us free from the law? What was the result of Christ "bearing the curse in our place" on the cross (3:14)?

Experience the Heart of God

- It seems clear in chapter 3 that the Galatians misunderstood the nature of the grace gospel and the meaning of Christ's crucifixion. Is there anything about the gospel and the Christian faith that you don't understand or have misunderstood in the past?

- How do you think it might look in your life to "turn from living in the Spirit to becoming slaves again to your flesh" (3:3) as you seek to experience the heart of God?

- How does it make you feel to know that it was God's plan all along to save people through the revelation of faith? And to know that the "the blessing of Abraham's faith is now our blessing too" (3:9)?

- How might it look today, in your life, to live in bondage to the legalistic rules of religion? In what ways have you tried to achieve "the righteousness of God by attempting to keep the law" (3:11) as you've sought to experience the heart of God?

- On a scale of 1 to 10, consider your experience of the heart of God right now. How much are you relying on the Holy Spirit to bring you to maturity in the Anointed One?

Share the Heart of God

- Like the Galatians, many in our culture are confused about the gospel of grace and the meaning of Jesus' death on the cross. How might you bring clarity to those in your life by sharing the heart of God found in the grace gospel?

- Consider people in your own life who are trying to experience God's heart. How many of them are trying to do so by keeping religious laws? How might sharing the gospel of grace liberate them and draw them closer to the heart of God?

- Galatians 3:8–9 tells us of God's plan from the beginning to rescue and re-create the world. How should this knowledge compel us to share the heart of God with others?

- Read 3:13–14 again. Why are these verses such good news for people you know who need to experience the heart of God?

CONSIDER THIS

At the heart of the grace gospel is the revelation-truth that we're made right with God by what *he* has done for *us*. Perhaps this idea that no one gets right with God by keeping religious rules is foreign and frustrating to you. Hopefully you've gained another perspective now. Jesus freed us from the curse of the law so we can serve and love God without the fear of not doing enough.

Lesson 5

The Purpose of the Law

GALATIANS 3:15-29

*Why then was the Law given? It was an intermediary
agreement added after the promise was given to show men how
guilty they are! It remained in force until the Joyous Expectation
was born to fulfill the promises given to Abraham.*
(Galatians 3:19)

One of the more difficult aspects of our faith is relating what God did
in the Old Testament to what he did through Jesus in the New Testament,
especially regarding the works of the Law. We have explored the tension of
faith and works in the past few lessons, learning that no one is made right
with God by trying to keep the Law. Why was it given at all, then? Good
question!

In our lesson today, Paul explores more of the tension of faith and works
by explaining why the Law was given in the first place. As he reveals, it was
always meant to be temporary. It was God's gracious gift to reveal sin and
help people join themselves to him in relationship—but only for a time. The
true unveiling of God's grace ultimately came with Jesus, where the gift of
faith outside of works now covers and clothes us in his anointing.

In Christ, the previous religious regulations, and the idea of a religious system governing and guarding people, have been set aside. Since the revelation of faith for salvation has been released, the Law is no longer in force and we are united with Christ in perfect freedom.

Discover the Heart of God

- After reading Galatians 3:15–29, what did you notice, perhaps for the first time? What questions do you still have? What did you learn about the heart of God?

- In 3:17–18, Paul makes a few observations about the Law and covenant (or royal proclamation) between God and Abraham. What did he reveal?

• What reason did Paul say the Law was given? How did he say it was given?

• How did Paul describe the Law and its rule in our lives until the revelation of faith for salvation was released?

• What have we become in Jesus, the Anointed One? What role did faith play in this? How does this impact the distinctions between people?

Explore the Heart of God

- In 3:15 Paul used an illustration of a contract to explain the promises of God to Abraham and the interaction of the Law and grace. Explain what Paul meant by this illustration. Why is it significant that the Law was given to Moses 430 years after God signed his covenant with Abraham?

- According to Paul, why do we receive the promises of the kingdom and the inheritance of God? What are those promises, and what do we inherit?

- Paul asked a good question in our reading: "Why was the Law given?" (3:19). How did Paul answer this question? What has faith done that the Law could not do?

- Why is it that the Law is no longer in force when faith comes into our hearts?

- How should 3:28 influence and impact church unity?

Experience the Heart of God

- Paul makes it clear in this passage that God always intended for us to relate to himself through his Son, Jesus, rather than through religious laws. How should this realization impact your experience of the heart of God?

- Paul proclaimed that we all enjoy the promises of God's kingdom realm because of our unity with the Anointed One, not because of religious laws or duty. Are you trying to experience the heart of God through religion rather than relationship? Explain.

- The Law and the promise (grace) each have a distinct function. The law brings conviction of sin, which unveils grace as the way to salvation. The law moves us, even compels us, to reach for grace. And grace will cause us to soar even higher than the demands of the law. How should this insight impact how we experience the heart of God?

Share the Heart of God

- Lots of people nowadays try to reach God's heart through fulfilling religious laws and duties. In what way might this lesson be useful as you share the heart of God with others?

- What are all the promises of the kingdom that are available to the people in your life? Make a list so you're ready to share them when you share the heart of God.

- How might 3:28 be important to your relationship with people as you share the heart of God with them?

CONSIDER THIS

We might shake our heads at Peter misleading the believers and his hypocrisy, yet don't we follow in his footsteps when we trade the revelation of grace for the religion of laws? We've learned from Paul that we make such a trade when we add religious regulations to the message of grace. Remember that we only receive God's righteousness by faith in Jesus, not by keeping the law.

Lesson 6

From Slaves to God's Children

GALATIANS 4:1–20

Now we're no longer living like slaves under the law,
but we enjoy being God's very own sons and daughters!
And because we're his, we can access everything our Father has—
for we are one with Jesus the Anointed One! (Galatians 4:7)

Slavery is a powerful word, conjuring up all sorts of images of men, women, and children being sold as property, forced into hard labor and toil, and held in bondage and restricted freedoms. So it's interesting that in today's lesson, Paul describes religious service using the same type of language.

You see, certain Christians in Paul's day were trying to add the religious regulations of Judaism to their new faith in Christ. Paul described such practices in this way: these people were "enslaved under the regulations and rituals of religion" (4:3), and they were "held hostage to the written Law" (4:5). Living under the law is like "living like slaves" (4:7), and adding religious rituals to faith is "the bondage of religion" (4:10). It's no wonder Paul was "truly dumbfounded" over what they were doing.

We might also be tempted to shake our heads at such willing enslavement. Yet how often are we compelled to add to the grace gospel in similar ways? By requiring people to experience certain baptisms, practice certain spiritual gifts, or observe certain religious rituals, we can be in danger of going "backwards into the bondage of religion" (4:10).

Instead of slaves, Paul reveals we're something remarkably better.

Discover the Heart of God

- After reading Galatians 4:1–20, what did you notice, perhaps for the first time? What questions do you still have? What did you learn about the heart of God?

- What did God do when the previous era of religious regulations and rituals came to an end?

- Paul said that before we knew God as Father we lived one way, then after knowing him we live in another way altogether. What are these two ways?

- How did Paul describe going back into the bondage of religion?

- Paul mentioned the work of false teachers in the midst of the Galatian Christians. What were they teaching and doing? What did they want from the people?

Explore the Heart of God

- According to Paul, how were we "juveniles"? What changed this state? Why has that era come to an end?

- Why did God send his Son "born of a woman and born under the written Law"? Why has he released the Spirit of sonship into our hearts?

- There is no requirement for Gentiles to become like Jews and observe Jewish ordinances in order to draw closer to God. Our approach is always on the basis of grace and faith in the blood of Jesus Christ. Yet in our reading, Paul suggested that the Galatians were returning to "the bondage of religion" (4:10). In what ways were the Galatian Christians seemingly going backward into bondage? Why was Paul so alarmed?

- Why did Paul tell the Galatian Christians to be like him and follow his example? What example was he giving them? Why would it help them?

- What did it mean that Paul was agonizing in "spiritual 'labor pains'" (4:19) over the Galatian Christians?

Experience the Heart of God

- Do you realize, deep down, that there is something better than religious regulations and rituals—*relationship* with God through Jesus? How should that realization impact how you experience the heart of God?

- How does it make you feel to know you've received your "freedom and a full legal adoption" as God's child because of his Son (4:5)? How might your life change if you fully lived and leaned into this reality?

- In light of the love of God, Paul is right: "Why would we, even for a moment, consider turning back to those weak and feeble principles of religion, as though we were still subject to them?" (4:9). Why do you think Christians turn back to religious duty? Have you ever done so in trying to experience the heart of God?

- How might it look in our day to "go backwards into the bondage of religion," as Paul implies in 4:10? What about following Paul's example of freedom?

Share the Heart of God

- Why is 4:3–5 such hopeful news for people you know? Why should it sit at the center of sharing the heart of God?

- In this reading, Paul invites people to follow his example and find freedom from the bondage of legalistic religion. How might it look to live in such a way that people in your life could follow your example into the same freedom?

- Who in your life do you need to "agonize in spiritual 'labor pains'" (4:19) for until the Anointed One is fully formed in them?

CONSIDER THIS

The Law of the old Jewish religious system was only a temporary solution in God's mission to rescue and re-create the world. So, as Paul questioned, "Why would we, even for a moment, consider turning back to those weak and feeble principles of religion, as though we were still subject to them?" (4:9). We aren't, because we're no longer slaves; rather, we are children of God!

Lesson 7

Life in Slavery vs. Life in Freedom

GALATIANS 4:21-31

*It's now so obvious! We're not the children
of the slave woman; we're the supernatural sons
of the freewoman—sons of grace!* (Galatians 4:31)

In which way would you rather live: slavery or freedom? This isn't a trick question. Obviously, none of us would want to be the property of another person and live in obedience to him or her. Yet Paul explains, as we'll see in our lesson today, that's exactly who we are when we turn to religious rituals to make us right with God.

He turns our attention to two Old Testament characters in order to illustrate this: Hagar and Sarah. The original context isn't important, though both were wives of Abraham who had covenantal arrangements with God. What's important is how Paul used them to establish a contrast between the law and Christ, slavery and freedom.

Paul traced two separate lines: one from Hagar to Ishmael to Mount Sinai to earthly Jerusalem to false gospel proponents; the other from Sarah to Isaac to Mount Zion to heavenly Jerusalem to the grace gospel. His con-clusion? Believers are children of the free woman, so we must not return again to the slavery of living under the law of religious rules and regulations. And since we are children of the free woman, we are heirs of the heavenly promises in Christ.

Discover the Heart of God

- After reading Galatians 4:21–31, what did you notice, perhaps for the first time? What questions do you still have? What did you learn about the heart of God?

- Paul opened our reading in today's lesson with three questions. What are those three questions?

- Whom did Paul say Ishmael and Isaac represent? How about Hagar and Sarah?

- Who is our true "mother"? Who are "the true children who inherit the kingdom promises" (4:28)?

- Of whom are we the children? Of whom *aren't* we the children of?

Explore the Heart of God

- What did Paul mean in 4:21-22 with his question about going back "to living strictly by the Law"? How would that look in your life today?

- Paul compared the stories of Ishmael to Isaac, and Hagar to Sarah, as another illustration about the law and grace. What was his point?

- Paul quoted Isaiah 54:1 in his discussion about the law and grace. How does it relate to his final illustration? How does this verse relate to us and our experience of the heart of God?

- How did 4:28–30 relate to the crisis situation facing the Galatian Christians, which alarmed Paul so much that he wrote his letter?

- What did Paul mean by his declaration "We're not the children of the slave woman; we're the supernatural sons of the freewoman— sons of grace" (4:31)?

Experience the Heart of God

- How do you think it would look to go back to living strictly by the law? Do you ever find yourself trying to live this way?

• In 4:26 Paul is showing that the law is a system of works, which brings bondage, and the promise is a system of grace, which brings true freedom. Which system do you find yourself living in these days?

• Paul declared that we have been birthed into freedom. As you've encountered the heart of God, do you feel free? Why or why not?

• How should 4:31 impact your day-to-day experience of the heart of God?

Share the Heart of God

- Have you found that most of the people in your life are living as sons of Hagar or sons of Sarah?

- How might Paul's analogy of Ishmael, Isaac, Hagar, and Sarah, be helpful to people as you share the heart of God with them?

- Why is 4:31 such good news to those with whom you share the heart of God?

CONSIDER THIS

In Paul's day, certain Christians were compelled to go back to living by their strict religious laws. And yet Paul reminded them that such living isn't freedom but slavery. Nowadays certain Christians are compelled to add religious regulations to the grace gospel. May we be reminded of the revelation-truth that in Christ we are children of the free woman—children of grace.

Lesson 8

Complete, Wonderful Freedom in the Anointed One

GALATIANS 5:1–12

Let me be clear, the Anointed One has set us free—
not partially, but completely and wonderfully free!
We must always cherish this truth and stubbornly refuse
to go back into the bondage of our past. (Galatians 5:1)

The apostle Paul opens our lesson with remarkable revelation-truth: Jesus Christ, the Anointed One of God, has set us free. Not partially free. Not halfway or almost free. Not even 99.99 percent free. He has set us completely and wonderfully free! But free from what? Paul gives us a clue in our key verse: the bondage of our past religious rituals and regulations.

You see, religious rituals don't do what we think they do. Instead of leading to life, they lead to death; instead of freedom, there's bondage; instead of "making it," we find we've missed it. The grace gospel is different, though. In light of God's love-gift, we don't read our Bibles because we have to but because "the rarest treasures of life are found in his truth. ... Nothing brings the soul such sweetness as seeking his living words" (Psalm 19:10). We follow Jesus in obedience, not out of obligation but because Jesus is "gentle, humble, easy to please," and because it is in him that we find "refreshment and rest" (Matthew 11:29).

What we find in relationship with God, and what you'll discover in this lesson, is total, complete, wonderful freedom and joy. That's what makes the grace gospel so sweet.

Discover the Heart of God

- After reading Galatians 5:1–12, what did you notice, perhaps for the first time? What questions do you still have? What did you learn about the heart of God?

- To what degree has the Anointed One set us free? What does Paul command about the truth of our wonderful freedom?

- How did Paul say we inevitably act when we believe that religious regulations (e.g., circumcision) make us holy?

- What is required of people who believe that religious regulations and rituals will bring them closer to God?

- What happens and what matters when we're placed into the Anointed One and joined to him?

- Paul had some strong words in this section about religious "agitators." What did he say about them?

Explore the Heart of God

- How has the Anointed One set us "completely and wonderfully free" (5:1)?

- Why is it that holding on to religious regulations and rituals as a means of being made holy denies that Jesus, the Anointed One, is enough?

- Why must people fulfill every single one of the commandments and regulations of the law if they hold on to one of them? How do Christians who try to be made holy through fulfilling religious regulations and rituals cut themselves off from the Anointed One?

- Why don't religious regulations and rituals matter for people who have been joined with the Anointed One?

- What did Paul mean by his question "Is there no longer any offense over the cross?" (5:11). Why is the cross offensive at all?

Experience the Heart of God

- Do you cherish the truth that you are "completely and wonderfully free"? How can you live in a way that cherishes God's grace gospel every day?

- Do you think there is benefit in certain religious regulations and rituals to make you holy? Explain. How do you think they've impacted your experience of the heart of God?

- Paul said, "All that matters now is living in the faith that is activated and brought to perfection by love" (5:6). How do you think this looks? How can you live more in the faith that's been activated in you in order to experience the heart of God in a greater measure?

- Why might you be persecuted, like Paul, for living and leaning fully into the grace gospel?

Share the Heart of God

- What religious regulations or rituals do people hold on to now-adays? Why is 5:5–6 so crucial to sharing the heart of God with them?

- Who in your life—whether a Christian or a non-Christian—can you help live "in the faith that is activated and brought to perfection by love" (5:6)?

- Paul claimed that the cross is offensive in his rhetorical question in verse 11. How might that be true today, especially in our multi-faith religious climate and in light of the grace gospel?

CONSIDER THIS

Galatians is a freedom-drenched letter from heaven, straight from the heart of God. This is why Paul repeated what he'd been saying all along: Jesus has set us completely and wonderfully free! If it hasn't already, may this revelation-truth sink deep into your being. You are free—from religious duty, from working for God's love, and from legalistic rituals. All that counts is faith expressing itself through love.

———

The Self-Life vs. the Spirit-Life

GALATIANS 5:13–26

*As you yield freely and fully to the dynamic life
and power of the Holy Spirit, you will abandon the cravings
of your self-life. For your self-life craves the things that offend
the Holy Spirit and hinders him from living free within you!*
(Galatians 5:16–17)

Imagine two trees in a garden: one tree produces poisonous berries, thorns and thistles, and flowers that smell of dead fish; the other tree produces mouthwatering fruit, lushly flowing vines, and flowers that smell of honeysuckle. Which one would you crave? Which would you want your life to reflect?

In many ways, these two trees represent the two kinds of life Paul draws our attention to in today's lesson: the self-life and the Spirit-life. The self-life craves and produces things contrary to the Spirit-life, things like sexual immorality and lust, hatred and arguments, resentment and envy. Paul warns us "that those who use their 'freedom' for these things will not inherit the kingdom realm of God" (5:21).

Paul also tell us about the Spirit-life, which overflows with joy and an enduring patience. It expresses kindness-in-action and a faith that prevails. It is a life that bears a gentleness of heart and strength of Spirit. May we choose each day "to live in the surrendered freedom of yielding to the Holy Spirit" (5:25).

Discover the Heart of God

- After reading Galatians 5:13–26, what did you notice, perhaps for the first time? What questions do you still have? What did you learn about the heart of God?

- Paul said we are free. But what doesn't that freedom give us the excuse to do? Instead, what does our freedom in Christ mean?

- Every believer lives with two competing forces within his or her heart. What are they?

- What are the cravings of the flesh, the "self-life"? What does it impact, and what will happen to those who continue to indulge them?

- What are the cravings of the Holy Spirit? What is the harvest produced by the Holy Spirit?

Explore the Heart of God

- At the start of this reading, Paul both encouraged us in and warned us against our freedom in Christ. Explain what Paul is teaching here.

- What is the self-life? What role does the dynamic life and the power of the Holy Spirit play in it?

- Compare and contrast the "vice" and "virtue" lists Paul gives in 5:19-21 and 5:22-23. How do they match up to each other? How do each of the virtues in the second list answer the vices in the first list?

- What does it mean that we "have already experienced crucifixion"? How has our self-life been "put to death on the cross and crucified with Messiah" (5:24)?

- In this passage, Paul seems to say that the Holy Spirit defeats our self-life cravings. But then Paul says we're called to choose the life of the Holy Spirit over the self-life. Which is it? Or are both true? Explain.

Experience the Heart of God

- In what ways do Christians nowadays use their "freedom in the Holy Spirit" to "set up a base of operations in the natural realm" (5:13)?

- Paul described two dynamics working in us: the self-life and life of the Spirit. How have you seen these dynamics at work in your life? Which life do you think you're experiencing mostly right now?

- Paul listed several cravings of the self-life. Which do you struggle with the most?

- Paul also listed several fruits produced within us by the Holy Spirit. Which do you find most evident in your life right now? Of which do you long for a greater harvest?

- Paul made the remarkable claim that our old self-life died along with Christ at the cross, yet parts of it still wage war against us (see Romans 7:15–24). We're also called to choose to "live in the surrendered freedom of yielding to the Holy Spirit" (5:25). How would it look in your life right now to trust that your self-life has been crucified, and then to fully yield to the Holy Spirit in order to experience the heart of God in a greater measure?

Share the Heart of God

- Part of what it means to be free in the Holy Spirit is to use that freedom to love others rather than ourselves through self-indulgence. Whom can you love today to demonstrate the true freedom available through Christ?

- What one or two specific self-life cravings can you abandon for the sake of sharing the heart of God in the love of Jesus?

- Who in your life needs to experience for themselves the heart of God found in the freedom of the Holy Spirit? How might you lead them into this freedom so they too can abandon the cravings of the self-life?

- Why are the fruits produced by the Holy Spirit so important to sharing the heart of God? How might growing those fruits in your life lead people you know deeper into experiencing God's heart?

CONSIDER THIS

Yes, it is for freedom that Christ has set us free through our faith in him. But not just any freedom. We aren't free to crave and live the self-life; we're free to live, through the power of the Holy Spirit, as God intends us to live. We are free to live a life of "divine love in all its various expressions" (5:22).

Lesson 10

Plant Good Seeds

GALATIANS 6:1–18

*And don't allow yourselves to be weary or disheartened
in planting good seeds, for the season of reaping the wonderful
harvest you've planted is coming!* (Galatians 6:9)

Galatians is a letter about freedom—heaven's freedom. But that doesn't mean we can live however we want. No, this freedom is about living for something. The grace gospel tells us we've been freed from the law of religious duty as much as from the law of sin and death. Now that we don't have to work to earn God's favor, we are free to work for his glory.

Paul wants us to keep our eyes on this part of our new life in Christ as he closes his letter. This is because—let's face it—sometimes we can become weary living as Christ has called us to live. Producing the fruit Paul spoke of in the last lesson is easier said than done. And yet, not only are we called to plant the seeds of the Spirit-life, we're also invited to live by the transforming power of this new kind of life in full resurrection freedom.

So let's do what Paul encourages us to do in the full freedom and power of heaven: fulfill the work God has given us with excellence, plant the good seeds of the Spirit-life, and do our life-boasting in the cross of Christ.

Discover the Heart of God

- After reading Galatians 6:1–18, what did you notice, perhaps for the first time? What questions do you still have? What did you learn about the heart of God?

- What does love empower us to do?

- Paul offered a sort of parable for how we live that involves planting and harvesting. Describe his illustration.

- According to Paul, why were those who insist that Christians be circumcised trying to recruit others to their side?

- In what did Paul boast? Why didn't circumcision and other religious regulations mean anything to him? What was meaningful instead?

Explore the Heart of God

- In our day, pointing out people's faults and calling them "fallen" isn't looked upon too highly. And yet Paul instructed us to do so with fellow believers. How is "restoring" them in this way one of the best ways we can love them?

• Explain Paul's parable about planting and harvesting when it comes to the self-life and the Spirit-life.

• Paul encouraged believers to not allow themselves "to be weary or disheartened in planting good seeds" (6:9), because they will reap a harvest if they don't give up. What harvest is he referring to?

• What did it mean that Paul had been "crucified to this natural realm," and that the natural realm was dead to him and no longer dominated his life? What does that mean for us? What did Paul mean that he boasted in "the crucifixion of our Lord Jesus, our Messiah" (6:14)?

- How does it look to live by the transforming power of this wonderful new creation life?

Experience the Heart of God

- Have you ever known a believer who fell from a place of victory? Have you experienced that yourself? How might 6:1 have helped the situation?

- What do you think is both the general and the specific work God has given you to do? How can you devote yourself to fulfilling this important work?

- Consider the kind of seed you're planting and harvesting. Does it mirror the self-life (5:19–21), or does it mirror the Spirit-life (5:22–23)? How is planting and harvesting impacting your experience of the heart of God?

- Have you ever found yourself growing weary or disheartened in planting good seeds? Explain. What can you do to guard against this in order to fully experience the heart of God?

- How might it look in your life to only care about what Paul did: "living by the transforming power of this wonderful new creation life" (6:15)? How would that change how you live?

Share the Heart of God

- Is there anyone you know or have known who needs to experience the heart of God through the restoration Paul described in 6:1? If so, how might it look to share God's love in this way?

- How can God use you in someone's life to fulfill the law of the Anointed One by carrying their troubles?

- Paul said, "If you plant the good seeds of Spirit-life you will reap the beautiful fruits that grow from the everlasting life of the Spirit" (6:8). These "good seeds" would include speaking wise words, giving, and loving every day. How might it look to drop such "seeds" in your everyday life?

• What opportunity can you take advantage of to be a blessing to others, especially in order to share the heart of God with people—whether inside or outside of church?

• What effect might it have on your witness to the heart of God with others if you, like Paul, cared about nothing else than "living by the transforming power of this wonderful new creation life" (6:15)?

CONSIDER THIS

Sometimes it can seem like what matters to God is saying certain prayers at certain times of the day, attending services a certain number of times each week, or having certain spiritual gifts or performing specific spiritual works. Yet Paul reveals what really matters: living by the transforming power of our wonderful new creation life in Christ. This is what ultimately leads to the heart of Paul's letter: it was for freedom that the Anointed One set us free.

Encounter the Heart of God

The Passion Translation Bible is a new, heart-level translation that expresses God's fiery heart of love to this generation, using Hebrew, Greek, and Aramaic manuscripts and merging the emotion and life-changing truth of God's Word. If you are hungry for God and want to know him on a deeper level, The Passion Translation will help you encounter God's heart and discover what he has for your life.

The Passion Translation box set includes the following eight books:

Psalms: Poetry on Fire

Proverbs: Wisdom from Above

Song of Songs: Divine Romance

Matthew: Our Loving King

John: Eternal Love

Luke and Acts: To the Lovers of God

Hebrews and James: Faith Works

Letters from Heaven: From the Apostle Paul (Galatians, Ephesians, Philippians, Colossians, I & II Timothy)

Additional titles available include:

Mark: Miracles and Mercy
Romans: Grace and Glory
1 & 2 Corinthians: Love and Truth
Letters of Love: From Peter, John, and Jude (1, 2 Peter; 1, 2, 3 John; Jude)

THE
PASSION
TRANSLATION

thePassionTranslation.com

thePassionTranslation.com